Using Money

Sharon Coan, M.S.Ed.

I **earn** money.

I have bills.

I have coins.

I will **save** some.

I will **spend** some.

I spend some bills.

I save some coins.

I have some money.

Sort It!

1. Get some coins.

2. Get some bills.

3. Group them.

4. How many are in each group?

Glossary

earn—to get something for work you have done

save—to keep and not spend

spend—to use money to pay for something

Index

Your Turn!

Pretend you have five dollars. What will you do with it? Make a plan. Share your plan.

Consultants

Shelley Scudder
Gifted Teacher
Broward County Schools

Caryn Williams, M.S.Ed.
Madison County Schools
Huntsville, AL

Publishing Credits

Conni Medina, M.A.Ed., *Managing Editor*
Lee Aucoin, *Creative Director*
Torrey Maloof, *Editor*
Lexa Hoang, *Designer*
Stephanie Reid, *Photo Editor*
Rachelle Cracchiolo, M.S.Ed., *Publisher*

Image Credits: Cover, p.1 Andersen Ross/Getty Images; pp.2–3, 5, 8, 14, 17, 23 (top) Blend Images/Alamy; p.10 Blue Jean Images/Alamy; p.19 OJO Images Ltd/Alamy; p.13 Gabe Palmer/Corbis; p.22 KidStock/Blend Images/Corbis; p.16 Fuse/Getty Images; p.23 (bottom) Jose Luis Pelaez Inc/Getty Images; p.11 Tim Hall/Getty Images; p.12 Michael Newman/Photo Edit; p.9 Photo_Concepts/iStockphoto; All other images from Shutterstock.

Teacher Created Materials
5301 Oceanus Drive
Huntington Beach, CA 92649-1030
http://www.tcmpub.com
ISBN 978-1-4333-7349-7
© 2014 Teacher Created Materials, Inc.